perhaps SPACE bunny ~~patte~~ patterns

For Anne and Lee and Neal, who brought
this book to life. With gratitude. —S. L.-J.

For Erica, Betsy, and Space Cat —N.L.

Text copyright © 2019 by Sally Lloyd-Jones
Jacket art and interior illustrations copyright © 2019 by Neal Layton

Visit us on the Web! rhcbooks.com

Educators and librarians, for a variety of teaching tools, visit us at RHTeachersLibrarians.com

Library of Congress Cataloging-in-Publication Data is available upon request.
ISBN 978-0-399-55818-4 (hc)
ISBN 978-0-399-55819-1 (lib. bdg.)
ISBN 978-0-399-55820-7 (ebook)

The text of this book is set in 18-point Century Schoolbook.
The illustrations were rendered in mixed media.

MANUFACTURED IN CHINA
2 4 6 8 10 9 7 5 3 1
First Edition

LOOK! I WROTE A BOOK!

(AND YOU CAN TOO!)

By Sally Lloyd-Jones

Illustrated by Neal Layton

schwartz & wade books · new york

When you want to write a book,
first you need a Good Idea.

You can get one from:

BASICALLY, you can write ANY book you like.
EXCEPT here's what you have to know:
 • what you're talking about

For instance, if you are writing a book about dinosaurs
but you don't know any good dinosaur names
(like Diplodocus, Triceratops, or Stegosaurus)
or even how to spell Cretaceous,
no one will believe anything you say.

Here's what else you have to know:

    • who it's for

If you're writing a book for your grandma,
for example, but it's all about tractors and
dump trucks, she will be snoring because it is
NOT EVEN INTERESTING to her!

You should write about things grandmas LOVE.

Like The Olden Days.

Or tap dancing.

Or you.

If you're writing a bedtime book for babies,
you can't have scary monsters inside
or they will be screaming
and not sleeping.

(Plus you can't use big words like Fragile or Hilarious
because they won't understand.
You have to use only small ones
like blocks or bug.)

Next, you sit still and do Quiet Concentrating
and get all your crayons in a row.
You must also get:

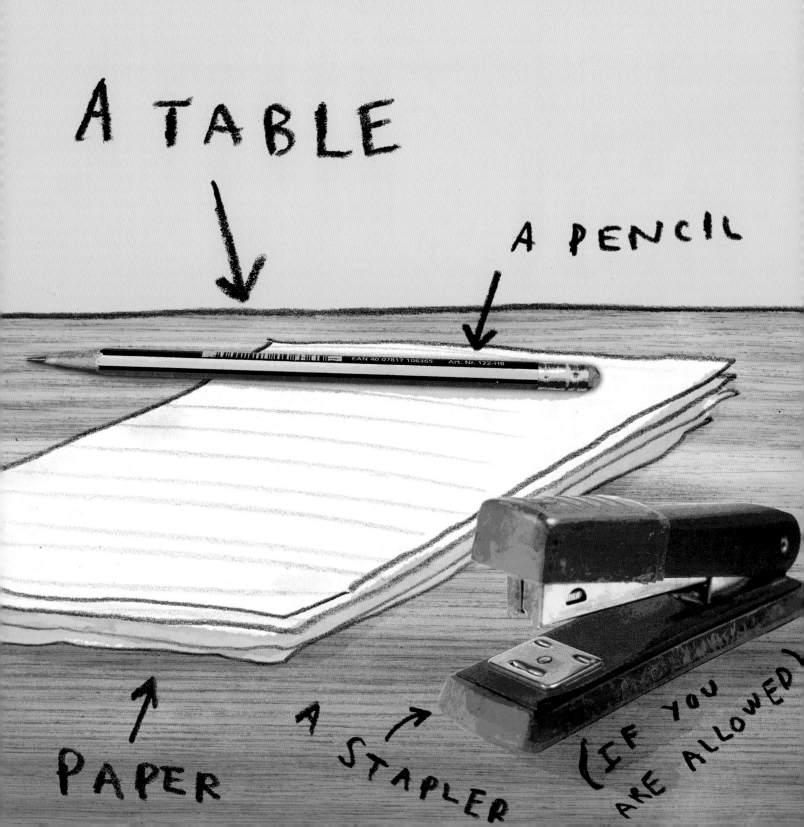

A TABLE

A PENCIL

PAPER

A STAPLER

(IF YOU ARE ALLOWED)

Now you need a title (which is what your story is called).
Here are some Good Titles:

(This is called a
How-To Manual.)

(This is a Horror Story.)

(This is a Tragedy.)

(This is a
History Book.)

(This is a Mystery.)

Here are some NOT good ones:

Remember, your title MUST be APPROPRIATE.
For instance, if your book is called Pretty Puppies
but inside are only horrible trolls,
readers could be disappointed.

Plus you DEFINITELY need a STORY.

Basically, a story has:

- a hero (like me)

- something she wants
(like maybe a horse)

- something stopping her
(like maybe a teacher or
a baby or a criminal)

- something happening
(She spies a horse in a field.)

• what goes wrong
(The horse runs away.)

• how she gets what she
wants in the end

(She finds the horse again and
tames it and rides home.)

At last, you're COMPLETELY
ready to start writing!
So you write a BEGINNING.
Here's a BAD beginning:

First we stood up.

Next we sat down.

(That would DEFINITELY win
THE MOST BORING BOOK EVER Prize.)

Here's a GOOD beginning:

Praying mantises have six legs and mandibles and
EAT THEIR HUSBANDS!

(This is nonfiction because you
ABSOLUTELY didn't make it up.)

Or:

A daddy had some children.
One day he lost them.

(This is fiction because you made it up.)

Then you write the MIDDLE, where all the stuff goes:

The daddy was worried. He looked everywhere. Where could he have put them?

After that you write the ENDING, which comes last:

Suddenly he found them.
They were hiding in the closet!
He was very happy. The End.

If you want people to cry, you write a sad ending:

Unfortunately, he DIDN'T EVER find them.
He was very disappointed. The End!

Always put **THE END** so everyone knows the story's over.
(If you put **TO BE CONTINUED...** everyone HAS to
read your next book.)

Now have your juice and snack.

You probably should have words AND pictures in your book.

If you have NO words, some people might not know what's happening and say, "I don't get it." And if you don't even have one picture, then it might send everyone to sleep.

When you're finished, you can show your book to your friends.

And they might say things like "This baby is not very fascinating" or "I think we need more bunnies in here."

Then you go away and draw better bunnies and cut
the part about the boring baby just sleeping.
Which means you REVISE it.
Which means it gets EVEN BETTER!

Now you stick the pages together
and make Page Numbers.
(You must be able to count.)

Next you draw your best picture with lots of colors in it
and it goes on the front,
and that's the Cover.

On the back you put what famous people thought of your book:

YOUR FRIEND'S NAME GOES HERE

"Anyone who doesn't read this is a cuckoo-head."

ABOUT THE AUTHOR

BLAH, BLAH BLAH, BLAH BLAH....

Then you make a beautiful portrait of yourself and underneath write About the Author and give Important Historical Facts, like:

- how old you are
- how many sisters and brothers you have
- your favorite color
- if you have a pet
- how many millions of cartwheels you can do without even stopping

Now you get people to buy your book. For instance, you could:

· be friendly

· give them cookies

· let them play with your trucks

· tie them to their chair

And that's how to write a Book and be an Author.

And then you just go back to being a normal person.

Or you could start your next book,

which is called a Sequel,

and write things like:

- How to Write ANOTHER Book
- THE RETURN of The Spiders On The Ceiling!
- The Daddy Who Lost His Children AGAIN!
- The Other Shoe... COMES HOME!

~~THE END~~